Steps To Good Governance

Dr. Marlene Street Forrest
Dr. Sylvan Lashley
Dr. Isaac Newton

ISBN: 9798853830042

Unfiltered Pages, Jamaica
Cover Design: DS Designs

Dedication

To every aspiring, new, tested, and retired leader searching tirelessly and courageously, to leverage the highest returns on your time, integrity, talent, and treasure. Your earnest efforts have touched and motivated us.

Acknowledgments

Our profoundest gratitude goes to the editor, Shanae Warburton, whose diligence made this book shine. We are grateful to Rochelle Simpson who brought the book to the finish line and got it published. We show appreciation to the creative genius of Abigail, Elizabeth and Matthieus Newton who masterminded the book cover and Demar Brown for providing such an attractive graphic design. To the many Prime Ministers, Presidents, Owners/Influencers, Board members, CEOs, Managing Directors and Leaders of countless government agencies, corporations, nonprofit, academic, and religious institutions in the Caribbean, North America, Latin America, Europe and Africa, your insistence, insights, struggles, stories, and successes have inspired this book.

To the Almighty God, without whose blessings and favour, naught would have been ventured nor achieved. To our many friends, families, colleagues, and readers, without your kindness, patience, support, encouragement, and blessings, this book would not exist.

Reviews

"Drs. Marlene Street Forrest, Sylvan Lashley, and Isaac Newton - three of the most skillful Caribbean minds with a global presence on good governance." – Dr. Haldane Davies, Professor of Practice in Higher Education and President of the University of the Commonwealth Caribbean.

"A fascinating take on how to align ethics, personal integrity and strategy for organizational success." – Olivia Lindsay, Founder and CEO of 876OnThe Go.

"Compelling, down-to-earth and practical." – Vere Hill, BBA (Fin.), MBA, FICB (Hons.), ACC. Dir. Managing Director of the August Group Ltd.

"The Decisions Board Members and CEOs make have real consequences for the failures and successes of their institutions. This book will inspire you!" – Suzy St. Brice, BA, LLC, MS, Senior Legal Officer for the Eastern Caribbean Securities Regulatory Commission.

"A timely book with fresh, helpful and probing insights on the folly of compromise and the importance of moral commitment for CEOs, Presidents and Board of Directors." – Dr. David Newton, MBA, MBBS, MD, Ph.D. Vice President of Greenville Medical Center, LLC.

"This book is remarkably useful for business executives, government officials, academic leaders, and non-profit presidents, whose decisions and actions require careful thought, planning and accountability for outstanding achievements." – Dr. Clinton Valley, Author, Leadership Professor and Former President of the University of Southern Caribbean.

"If followed carefully, leaders who put into practice this pioneering initiative, the moral influence of their decisions will undoubtedly impact unborn generations. Books like this are urgently needed." – Dr. Conroy Reynolds, Clinician, Professor, Author, and Theologian.

"Here is a meaningful, momentous, and mesmerizing treatment of good governance. It is laid out in a profound, perceptive, practical, and piercing plan of action

framework. User friendly to the core." – Dr. Howard Simon, Family Therapist, Author, Pastor, Poet, and Leadership Consultant.

"Drs. Street Forrest, Lashley and Newton deftly offer an infinitely more elegant marriage of ethical principle with professional practice. As wellness is great for the body so good governance is best for institutional health." – Dr. Suzette Henry, MBA, MBBS, MD, Ph.D. A practitioner that integrates faith, healing, dying, grief, and wellness.

"The authors' combined experience, effortless wisdom and distilled knowledge are practical, wise, and warm. This is a solid foundation for good governance from the heart, not just in the boardroom." – Beresford Mack, President of Tirandentes, LLC.

Table of Contents

Preface

What does it mean to be a CEO, President, Board Member, and Board Chairperson? Is there a clearly defined path to addressing cybersecurity, fraud, regulatory disruptions, political instability, and global financial crises? Are there tools, strategies, and dilemmas that invite arresting synergy between a productive CEO, the Entrepreneurial Owner, and a passionate Board Chairperson? These five (5) engaging, elegantly simple in style, but richly practical chapters, serve as reference points to the 'must-do' and 'stay-clear' factors of building a robust institution. They are premised on principles, policies, and practices of corporate good governance.

We have intended this offering to provide a brick-laying foundation for the newcomers who have been tasked with the serious responsibility of being a Board member, and for veterans who have embraced their perceptive responsibilities with balanced analysis and purposeful care. All leaders are encouraged to live positively expectant with uncertainty and to operate with high levels of flexibility. The authors advise that the surest way to turn this pioneering approach into a road map for adding value, driving growth, and adapting to change is to immerse oneself in the process. In a world littered with bankrupt companies, ever-changing technological advances, and public health cross-border drift of pathogens, leaders must become ethically minded, fiscally accountable, risk alert, legally aware, operationally nimble, and strategically focused.

These relevant concerns reflect the integrated external influences and institutional capabilities that thriving organizations must maneuver skillfully and intelligently. This book offers practical recommendations highlighting the urgency to apply good governance to ensure a more satisfying future - fiscally for the company and happiness generally for staff and customers.

The authors argue implicitly that good governance emerges from the belief that the boardroom is not the only place where mission, vision, and accountability are played out. It first resides in the conviction of the heart, the power of the will, and the courage to lead organizations with purpose.

In trying to navigate different voices in the good governance matrix, we identified multi-layered solutions drawing mainly from over 125 years of collective experience as Board Chairs in academic and corporate settings; Presidents of private businesses; Managing Directors of financial institutions; Lecturers in business; Writers of life-transforming books; and Leadership consultants.

Collective action, a sincere meeting of the minds, shared values, an ability to analyze facts, and a clear understanding of the mission, the organizational structure, and regulations, are imperatives which must be present. By taking ownership of these resources, leaders signal the surest way to DO and be adept at good governance, is to bring astonishing change, formidable exploration, and sustainable achievement. Good governance must be made into a daily practice.

This book is written to enrich your relationship with others in your organization and beyond. It ultimately reveals the true meaning of your essential values in shaping the contours of your company's future.

- Drs. MSF, SAL and IJN

Foreword

As Chairman of several national, regional, and global boards, having served as Prime Minister for 20 years, and now Minister of Foreign Affairs, I have had to be sensitive, mindful, dutiful, and committed to good governance. More than a guiding operational principle, good governance has always been a fundamental attribute of my leadership, thinking, and being.

This book is an excellent review of issues relating to good governance, with a broad ambit encompassing all aspects of organizational planning, purpose, and achievements. One unique feature of this book is that each chapter is a stand-alone and can be read according to the reader's specific interest. Each of the three authors has presented thoughts in the chapters that are weaved effortlessly into the fabric of the good governance model explored.

Too much is at stake when global best practices are violated. However, when leaders: Board Directors, Board Chairmen, CEOs, Presidents, and Departmental Heads employ them in daily usage, the gain is indisputable.

Explanations of varying models of good governance, coupled with graphic illustrations of concepts presented and cases depicting actual lived experiences, are succinctly covered. Issues of an ethical, regulatory, accountability, and strategic nature, are specific to the book's focus. These all match to high-yielding solutions.

Steps to Good Governance is not intended to be used to recall facts and/or the definition of terms. Instead, the authors hope that its conceptual design will be a guidepost that will contribute to preserving the sustainability of companies, especially as they adjust to both internal and external changes. The core thesis is that synergy must be established between Board Chairmen, Owners/Influencers, and CEOs/Presidents, for institutions to remain flexible, responsive, nimble, vibrant, efficient, fiscally prudent, robust, and stable, meanwhile critically staying relevant to their brand, their customers, workers, partners, and stakeholders.

Oftentimes, leaders ignore moral impulses to the great detriment of their companies. The challenge is not that good governance is burdensome, but simply that there is the proclivity to place an overemphasis on impressive prosperity, to miscalculate risks, and disguise abject personal greed, which can lead to, inter alia, abuse of the environment, political machinations, and a rapid turnover of workers. Additional downsides are the tarnishing of the companies' brand and possible inimical legal consequences. All could emerge if keen attention to durable values is not actively maintained. Adherence to good governance tempers unethical tendencies and places the wellness of organizations above all other priorities.

The authors have, cumulatively, over 125 years of experience in the service of offering grounded, solutions-oriented, and high-performance advice in a variety of settings. They have set out a bold, innovative, and clear framework of what constitutes good governance and how it must be harnessed. For leaders who are beginning their journeys, those at the height of their careers, those on the farewell stage of retirement, or those on the retired mentoring seat, good governance is the only condition for stunning organizational productivity, longevity and thriving.

In this light, few other writers have so poignantly put the pieces on the table of behaviours and practices requisite for good governance, as these authors. They have done this in a culturally constructive and responsible manner, which minimizes potential risks. Even as leaders strive for greater clarity and probity, the practical value of this book is immense. Drs. Street Forrest, Lashley, and Newton deliver a winning introduction to good governance that each of you will enjoy.

- The Rt Hon. Dr. Denzil L. Douglas, Minister of Foreign Affairs, International Trade, Industry, Commerce and Consumer Affairs, Economic Development, and Investment. Dr. Douglas is the former PM of St. Kitts and Nevis (1995-2015).

Chapter 1

Corporate Governance At A Glance

Corporate Governance At A Glance

What is Good Governance? The question has plagued generations and dozens of definitions abound. Here, we share our perspectives as citizens of developing countries. *"Like the eye of an eagle, the reflection of a mirror and the oil in a car, good governance makes organizations see ahead, examine their values and work well — we look to the future."*

The concept of governance arises out of American frontier history where the entire community gathered to determine the smallest matters. There was the birth of states' rights and federal rights, leading to the famed 'Separation of Powers' concept, a balance between local, state, and federal government — it's a balance of power. Yet, we must deal with the present to keep an oversight on all that happens. We have copied much of this history in our present structures and cultures as we strive to integrate oversight, representation, freedom to act, and goodwill, with power and influence to deliver in the present. Our thesis is that governance is birthed in our history to integrate a balance of power/influence with future hope and present reality.

Vision of the Future

"Good governance, then, represents the wisdom of establishing policies, practices, and a philosophy that enables institutions to flourish beyond those who founded or started them. If looking towards the future is unsure and the present compromised, good governance is either abandoned, does not exist, or is not understood. However, when companies are growth-oriented, they preserve their purpose by creating a culture of innovative success premised on integrity."

-   Dr. Isaac Newton

Operational Efficiency

"Good governance is where a company establishes a framework that allows for the smooth functioning of all aspects of the organization, which lends itself to transparency, ethics, compliance, accountability, and transformation. Established by the Board, the guiding principles enable the organization to coalesce around common goals and values, resulting in behaviour that is free from conflict of interest and has the guardrails that allow for checks and balances, including a responsive mechanism to address conflicts and non-compliance."

- Dr. Marlene Street Forrest

Power/Influence Balance Sharing

"Good governance is that conscious sharing of power/influence between owners/influencers, CEOs, and Chairs, that rests on legal, ethical, and professional accountability wrapped into policies and procedures, structures, and functions, and devolving into an inclusive and diverse group called a Board. It is a system brokered by the titans of power and influence in shared triad arrangements of CEO, Owner/Influencer and Board Chair, emanating from the historical context and culture of the governed, and those governing, and culminating in present practice."

- Dr. Sylvan A. Lashley

In summary, good governance, a combined and integrated system of Board composition, Board regulation, and Board execution, is impacted by the historical and cultural context of the society as a base point, proceeds into the structure of functions, and roles in the present, and steps toward the future with a keen eagled eye. Our main thesis is that good governance is characterized by history and context, as a basis for role and function, and with projection to aspiration and vision, schematized by three triangular representations, culminating into a 9-sided polygon or nonagon, called an enneagram, and displayed visually below.

Nine-Sided Nonagon (Enneagram)

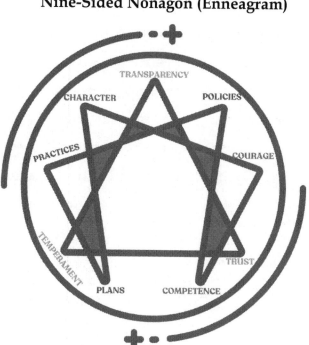

3T's—Trust, Transparency, Temperament

3P's—Plans, Policies, Practices

3C's Competence, Character, Courage

3 (T+P+C) (History + Present + Future) = Execution and Results

We hold firm that any definition of good governance must exist within a historical, political, social, and economic context of those to be governed, and those who would govern. Utilizing this assumption, then good governance can vary based on the socio-political and economic context of the governed. Good governance is an agreed-upon operative, systematic framework of procedures, regulations, and roles among power bloc stakeholders who permit a representative body of individuals to act on behalf of the whole in a fiduciary and legal manner, with respect to history, cultural context, moment, vision, mission, strategy, and results.

Good governance delivers the accountability framework that drives an organization to deliver on the dreams and visions, aspirations and hopes of the constituted body. Thus, good governance combines politics, competence, policies, values, diversity, inclusion, and equity. Ultimately, good governance is a brokered power arrangement, rather formally or informally, consciously, or subconsciously, between the CEO representing the executive team, the Board Chair representing the full Board, and 'Owner/influencer' groups that may or may not be on a Board.

Several governance models come to mind. The authors offer a new approach to Board governance in the proposed trio model where the major connecting points of the Board Chair, CEO and Owner/Influencer, become the triangular Board of the future. Each trio point represents a power source. Here are our governance models:

1. The Political Model: The representative model, represents large constituent groups where Board members obtain their positions on the Board based on their representation of a group — we call this positional, referent power.

2. The Competency Model: The Board may lack the expertise and governance to develop the knowledge and skill of Board models — this is expert power.

3. The Policy Model: The Board is operated from a policy perspective with the Board of Governors as Chair. This includes the CEO and a few standing committees with the CEO as the main person — we refer to this as the executive power.

4. The Traditional: The Board speaks with one voice as per bylaws, and there are no sub-committees — this is traditional power.

5. The Valued Aspirations: The value the organization brings to the community — this is referred to as aspirational power.

6. The Cooperative Model: All Board members have an equal voice and vote to serve their constituents—we call this distributive servant power.

7. The Management team: The Board and organization are run by a management team of the CEO and Board members---this is called management power.

8. The Trio Model: Board Chair, CEO, Owner/Influencer incorporation—this model combines several prior features of politics, competence, policies, shareholder representation, and values leading to structure and function. This model asserts that power and influence are brokered among the Board Chair, the CEO, and the Owners/Influencers, to written agreements of each person's responsibilities and duties, and pictures a silent owner/influencer in the background—we call this brokered trio power.

We advise that individuals first study and assess their political, social, economic, and legal environment and context, determine whether their organizations are non-profit or for-profit, and then pinpoint the location and distribution of power sources. It is important to adopt a trio approach so that power is brokered by agreement among the principal parties to determine who does what and when. It is possible that more than three sources of power may appear in location, but we classify them under CEO power, Chair power and Owner/Influencer power. It is evident that Boards in developing countries must be cognizant of the sources of power in their environment, and be attuned to the voice of the people, the voice of the government, and the voices of the owners/influencers. It is awareness of these combined voices that will augur for progress and positive results, for, *"Can three walk together except they be agreed?"*

Chapter 2

The Strategic Role Of The Board

The Strategic Role Of The Board

Unpredictable change and alarming uncertainty are factors cutting across cultural norms and proven conventions at a rate and speed that is upending global realities. This is happening in ways that are politically disruptive, financially volatile, technologically dependent, public health frightening, religiously fragile, and socially unsettling. In facing the real consequences of this shifting environment, leaders of corporations, owners/influencers, and chairpersons of Boards must look past zero-sum approaches to negotiation.

The days of instant gratification, which demand meeting profit thresholds and overlooking good governance behaviours, are numbered. If leaders fail to pivot leveraging the opportunity for positive change, diffusion of innovative energies will push companies out of the marketplace. With fresh eyes and new commitments, cultures of resistance are rubbing up against the need to embrace change without a familiar guide toward successful outcomes.

Real attention to purpose and strategy requires that Board chairpersons, owners/influencers, and CEOs work from different perspectives with the same sets of core values-empathy to engage external customers and partners with compassion to meet work-life objectives of internal customers without offending stakeholders' interests, whether dealing with new markets, new products/services or restructuring internal processes, how to find strategic balance in moments where decisions require paying imbalanced attention to critical priorities is a struggle. These include aligning tasks with talent versus identifying a clear pathway forward; improving customer engagement while maximizing internal information flow without sacrificing diversity; and working with influencers to discover better solutions and situating open-door synergies between the Board chairpersons, owners/influencers, and CEOs.

Strategic thinking and acting flow from several essentials. These are cultivating the right mindscape, providing critical support, and executing with excellence.

1. <u>Cultivating the Right Mindscape</u>

One of our parents once said, "*Son, focus on the one important aspect that makes this beautiful mango fruit tree bloom and blossom. If you do, you'll always be eating mangoes as long as you live.*" Applied to good governance, there should be a single mindscape reflecting a shared standard so that leaders can function in a high-stake, ever-changing environment. Values that stabilize, principles that run deep, and convictions that breathe consistency, will always yield an abundance of good fruits.

To achieve this mindscape, leaders must enter the world within their thinking and imagination. This is a drilling process. Board chairs, owners/influencers, and CEOS must ask the right questions on both sides of the corporate table: the strategic, supportive, and monitoring board side, and the operating result-driven side.

Why is the mission of our company important? What hidden challenges must we identify to effect short-term and long-term changes? What connecting experiences do we need to cement mutual trust? How do we know if what we are doing is effective or useless? Can we sense when the time is right to make relevant adjustments? What is adding value to our organization?

Are we sure about our strengths and areas of growth, and clear about the impact our decisions will have on our employees, clients, customers, partners, and stakeholders?

Digging deeper is vital to clarify core, unshakable principles, that inform and guide good governance beliefs. Leaders bring different moral assumptions that make the experience of serving their organizations purposeful. These also provide an effective means to build consensus around a set of agreed upon criteria for discussions and interactions, which could lead to mutually acceptable collective action. While common sense, intelligence, and optimism can drive goals, it takes values to craft a unity of purpose. Several values constitute a sense of duty and responsibility that is greater than oneself. They are the well from which strategic water will spring forth.

Candid Honesty: While it is necessary to search for common ground, often, an opposing viewpoint that challenges the unity of opinion can break up taken-for-granted assumptions, clear up unspoken fear, and foster candour. Nothing that enhances or retards the mission of the organization should be off the discussion table. Being honest is better than staying silent. Constructive criticisms can give birth to the hidden reasons behind vital decisions to be decided immediately and in the future.

Openness to Learning: This value is critical because it forces leaders to be alert to their mistakes, misjudgments, and possible errors. Knowing that you can get it wrong means that you are more willing to learn both from what went off course and what is working well. What is important is learning the right lessons by comparing good and bad outcomes for a more comprehensive understanding of the next steps. Shared Accountability: Leaders must agree to take ownership of their collective responsibility to each other and the organizations they serve. Each should value the greater cause to which all are called to defend. It takes courage to safeguard your integrity. If you want to make a difference, you must bring your entire being to the table and know the legal, financial, and moral obligations you have to your organization.

Inclusiveness: Embarking on a journey of integrating and engaging diverse individuals, voices, and viewpoints, is an essential value. It opens the door for leaders to act based on careful planning and make decisions that drive change through influence. Leaders must demonstrate a desire to listen to the concerns, priorities, misfortunes, and successes of others. This can usher in greater creativity in solving problems and finding sustainable solutions together. Intentional inclusion that questions our personal biases matters.

Resourcefulness: Leaders must bring maximum attention to their companies. They must channel their gifts, talents, expertise, and experiences to build connections. Taken as a whole, these contribute to shared vision and responsibility. Each leader must answer: How is my participation protecting the well-being of this organization?

Humility: Being humble requires head, heart, and shoes. This means valuing those around you to the point that you can understand what is informing how they are thinking (head), empathizing with what they are feeling (heart), and putting yourself in their place (shoe). These three approaches allow leaders to connect with others, build healthy relationships, and more easily resolve conflicts. Intolerance for Mediocrity: Leaders should read materials sent to them after and before meetings, attend meetings regularly and on time, and ask critical questions about issues to be decided. They must display enthusiasm to serve willingly and demonstrate the energy, motivation, and commitment to perform their duties with excellence. There must be zero tolerance for mediocrity.

2. <u>Providing Critical Support</u>

Good governance is inescapable. Bad governance erodes standards of institutional excellence. Good governance does not occur in mid-air. Companies pay a high price when ethical practices and accountability ideals fail. Yet, good governance functions best from the interplay of cultivating the right mindscape and the art of strategic support. Organizations are not looking for spotless leaders. They are interested in genuine leaders who can plan for the future, solve the issues before them creatively, and demonstrate a permanently teachable spirit. These strategic exercises keep leaders engaged, stimulated and creative in providing strategic support.

Plan for the Future

To think of planning for the future, some of us readily assume the obvious: that we can predict outcomes with a certain degree of probability. The truth is that we do not know all the variables or combinations of factors that can dent our sharpest strategic plans. We must be prepared to simply go on a journey from where we are, to where we imagine going. The most vital question that board members can ask in providing strategic support to presidents and CEOs is this: In the next three years, and three years after that, how could this organization bring more benefits to our employers, customers, partners, and shareholders? To nail this question with greater precision, ask and answer: What is the fastest, most direct path to deliver spectacular results to all those we are dedicated to serving?

Before Board leaders examine the hard facts, real figures, and solid evidence that will help them both review internal resources and examine how external challenges could be filtered to improve the forward-thrusting journey, they must discard blind loyalty to current people to whom they owe favours and unreasonable fear of the unknown. These two tendencies will stifle and undermine a vision of the future guided by a commitment to the company's mission and a conscience that is ready to support the right decision.

Problem Solve Creatively:

Identifying the problem as a prerequisite for solving it is one of the ways Board members provide strategic support. During the height of the pandemic, an experiment was conducted with a brilliant young CEO and her Board of Directors from Jamaica. We divided the team into two groups of five persons each. The company was a technology driven transportation and logistics solution business. It was less than four years old and found itself in the middle of an unexpected global pandemic with the country under lockdown.

At the time, a vaccine had not yet been developed. Although the company was using the latest cutting-edge technology that enabled the public to book cabs, eliminated cash payments, and provided greater security coverage for both passengers and drivers, only essential workers were permitted access to the roads. The island's tourism was crippled. Schools were closed. Social isolation was in full effect, and the terrifying fear of the Covid-19 contagion was spreading like wildfire. The big problem was whether leaders should close down the company since no reliable data was available to predict when operations would return to normal or look for innovative ways that the company could scale up its transportation services to achieve growth. Using electronic communications, we asked both groups to clarify the problem. Group one discussed for only ten minutes per day for two days, the consequences of the company choosing not to act.

Group two, using the same period, framed the problem around one question: What is the scope of the market? We found that 81 percent of leaders in Group one demonstrated positive responses to being flexible in taking risks, searching for cracks in the system, and identifying targeted rewards.

The second group recorded only 51 percent positive responses. On further probing, leaders who concentrated on the scope of the market reflected a lesser number of positive responses; they were more willing to wait on reliable data to determine when drivers should return to work.

Alternatively, the group that examined the cost of not acting showed ingenuity by combining passion, keen reasoning, and a sense of creative urgency. This group left ample room for a new business model to emerge from the pandemic chaos. These pivoted to transporting essential workers and delivering food to senior citizens' homes. Board leaders who were open to problem-solving creatively were more concerned with getting buy-in from each other to take action that could make a difference. They were more prone to spot opportunities for stakeholders, workers, and consumers, that would directly benefit them. By clarifying and simplifying the problem, Board members were better able to generate the best ideas and prioritize them. Approaching ideas from different perspectives induced a surprising process that yielded new solutions.

Possess A Permanently Teachable Spirit:

There is no single formula for embracing a permanently teachable spirit. One way is to think of stories. They foster creativity, relevance, and connectivity. We enjoy listening to them and we love telling a powerful story. They make us laugh, cry, think and aspire. Create in your organization a teachable space to keep on learning, not just on an occasional moment, but as the norm in which your institution operates. Then think like a storyteller. Make the issues you care about memorable, specific, and meaningful. Two principles are helpful to keep your mind always ticking with new possibilities for learning as a Board leader.

An old pastor once remarked, "If you want to keep your members fascinated with your preaching either tell a new story or tell an old story new." This simple advice produces a teachable spirit.

Another renowned senior pastor in an inner city in the USA invited our team to the church Board. They wanted to increase the men's membership since the church had 89% women in faithful attendance. We visited the surrounding targeted neighbourhood where the church was located. We asked who the men were, what were their needs and beliefs, and how could the church attract them. With the data in hand, we told Board members two stories.

First, we told a story about the church developing a reputation where men in the immediate community could become homeowners. The church would invest in making the men credit worthy. It will then organize them into real estate, interior design, plumbing, and painting groups reflective of their skill sets. Having assisted the men in buying their first homes through city auction, the men would agree to make a three-year contribution to any of the church's community outreach programs. The men also were to use their combined skill sets to upgrade the houses the church purchased.

The second story was crafted from a different angle. We shared how the church would invite the men to its food basket programs. Members would hold creative Bible Studies while offering each man security, cleaning, and cooking jobs. We asked Board members to imagine the impact these two activities would have on their membership growth prospects.

In the first story, the committee made up of mostly women, reported that they saw homeowners as potential spouses. They believed that the men would more likely become solid church members.

In the second story, the men were imagined as leaving the church after the jobs were completed. It was assumed that the men would have loosely held ties with the church. The church invested thousands of dollars into the homeownership program. Within three years, the Men's Ministry moved from a handful to over 200 men. Once leaders discovered how best the church could gain the men's loyalty by learning to meet their felt needs, returns on investments exceeded everyone's imagination.

Stories have the potential to inspire leaders to become teachable. Whenever leaders want to see old problems in fresh light or simply spot a new solution, story thinking and telling can lead to teachable discoveries.

3. Executing with Excellence

In order to execute with excellence, the Board must get a firm grip on what it means to complete a task. Be prepared to do it well, focus fully on the task to be achieved and take incremental steps that advance delivery to the finish line consistently until the mission is accomplished. Even after values cohere with strategic support, nothing will get done on the Board until it gets done. We have learnt that actions speak louder than words. However, words combined with actions speak loudest! Executing with excellence also means that actions must be fueled by shared values and mutual respect between the owner, influencer, Board chairman, and president/CEO.

Soft skills are crucial to getting things done efficiently. A combination of self-discipline, ambition, clarity about goals, timeline, and keen attention to the task at hand, are key factors to achieve proposed outcomes in a timely manner. Procedural intelligence allows for actions to be carried out, not perfectly but keenly, alertly, and with resilience. Periodically, the Board must step back and assess where the company, organization, or institution is, and the kind of action needed to narrow in on short-term and long-term goals. Collective action contains a bold and pragmatic roadmap. "Is this action aligning with our company's mission and priorities?", is a question which should be asked and answered. The Board will not act alone. It does so in concert with others, but it must be prepared to act in the midst of ambiguity, uncertainty, and complexity, and simultaneously find the simplest path to success. The Board's functions according to the Legal Practical Bylaws (LPB): Legally, the Board approves, disapproves, or adjusts the agenda proposed by the president/CEO and offers broad support for the organization's goals, projects, initiatives, and objectives. Practically, the president/CEO sets the operational agenda, makes recommendations to the Board, and implements decisions. Bylaws set the terms, boundaries, and criteria of what the company can do and cannot do. Another way to look at this is to understand that the Board accomplishes things in two ways:

1. Sub-committees, which are assembled around some specialized issues, vet these issues under consideration and engage in interchanges and exchanges, that lead to the consensus to be established in the larger Board meetings. Sub-committees also comprise of heads or

directors of the various departments. They help to coordinate priorities and clarify informational gaps.

2. The Board also gets things done through the organization's president or CEO. This person decides on the direction of the company; manages the policies, liabilities, and resources; implements plans and strategies; recommends decisions to be voted on the Board; navigates rapid changes and progress; authorizes and directs major departments; and establishes financial controls. He or she is the public face of the company. Informally, the Board facilitates other initiatives for engagement:

   - Philanthropic activities. These involve working and sharing with external leaders and organizations on charitable initiatives and long-term worthy social causes.

   - Networking with other businesses. Making connections could turn the organizational brand into something that gains higher visibility and impactful viability.

   - Community Services. These should be at the top of the list. They should always be in the well-being of the organization.

- Resources gathering and information sharing. Underline these activities. They will help Board members better appreciate what needs to be done, and how best to do it.

Only when attitudes and action steps come together will the board eventually spur innovative outcomes that will get things done excellently. The Biblical principle of reaping and sowing drives out complacency, false hope, finger-pointing, procrastination, and inaction. The future and present success of your organization is crafted along the line of each Board member providing strategic support. This demands personal choice and collective action. So, what is the answer? Take the first step towards the highest quality service!

Chapter 3

Guidelines For Optimal Efficiency

Guidelines For Optimal Efficiency

So, you have made the decision of incorporating your company. Congratulations! This is one of the first steps in ensuring that your assets are secured and that owners and directors understand their rights and the responsibilities they have to fellow shareholders, investors, and their statutory obligations. In most countries, you would have been incorporated under stated legislation and governed by a Companies Act. Corporate Governance begins here, as it is the duty and responsibility of directors to ensure that the company complies with the Act which establishes the framework within, and which directors and shareholders must operate, and if followed, will direct all directors to establish the required necessary board structures and committees through which directors can govern.

Every director must hold responsibility for discharging his/her duties under the Act, and in keeping with the documents of incorporation seriously, and must also hold other directors accountable. We use the term "fiduciary" to refer to such duties.

This chapter will consider several key administrative activities arising from many Companies Acts and Documents of Incorporation, that when established by directors will result in the proper discharge of their responsibilities and an enhanced governance framework. The objective for which the Company is formed, and which is formally set out in the Company's constitutive documents should be read and understood by each director, as it guides in establishing the mission of the company and the use of words with which a directors must become familiar. Words such as "establish", "ensure", "develop", "provide", "formulate", and "conduct", are frequently used in the raft of duties of a director and are usually associated with issues of governance. Directors are encouraged to focus on the following seven (7) major areas of responsibility:

1. Share Capital, Shareholders & Shareholdings

Here, the focus in governance should be in ensuring that there is a register of members which must record the number of shares held by each shareholder and provide information such as the shareholder's address and other information to allow for communication. There is a greater emphasis now on matters relating to money laundering and proceeds of crimes. Therefore, where there is a company or trust listed as a shareholder, provision should be made to record the beneficial shareholder(s).

Changes to capital allocation must be registered under the Companies Act, and the Board, through the Company Secretary or other delegated authority, must ensure that this process is observed. Share certificates which are given to shareholders to record ownership can be physical but are more often now provided in an electronic format through a central securities depository.

2. General Meetings

We have been nominated to the Board of Directors of the Company. Possibly, we are a shareholder-director, or we may be an independent director, but we are all here to discharge our responsibilities as directors to ensure the success of the company, act within the powers of the Articles of the Incorporation, exercise independent, collective skill and due diligence, and avoid conflicts of interest, as fiduciaries. The

Board must now consider the scheduling of Ordinary General Meetings, its Annual General Meeting (AGM) and other scheduled meetings of the Board of Directors. Typically, the first Annual General meeting is held within a year to 15 months of the company's incorporation.

At the Board of Directors meeting, Directors hold Management accountable for reporting on the strategic initiatives and general operations of the company. Equally, at the AGM, the shareholders hold you, the directors, accountable. You must report to them on the general governance of the company, through the committees established by the Board of Directors such as the Audit Committee or the Governance Committee. The Chairman, who is elected by other members of the Board of Directors, leads, and chairs the AGM.

Procedurally, a General Meeting can only be called if there is a Notice of Meeting which is specified in the Acts or laws of a country and in the constitutive documents. There are times, depending on the circumstances when shorter than normal notice is necessary and there is a provision for that as well. Upon sending out the Notice of the AGM, all shareholders on the register must be given sufficient time, usually at least 21 days' notice, in writing. Included in the

Notice of the General Meeting are the matters to be discussed and the resolutions that the shareholders will vote on and includes the acceptance of the Financial Statements, Directors, Remuneration of Directors, and the continuation in office of the auditors. Matters of capital or capitalization of the companies are usually addressed at these meetings as well. The Audited Financial Statements should also accompany the Notice of the AGM.

The role of the Company Secretary is very critical in ensuring an orderly meeting as the Secretary sends out the Notice, ensures that there is a quorum at the meeting, assists the Chairman in his role in presiding over the meeting, advises on the procedure if there is no Chairperson, and advises the meeting on the protocol for voting. The efficiency, validity and effectiveness of a meeting is enhanced by the attention to these details which are outlined in a company's Articles.

3. Directors

The Company determines the number of directors necessary to run the company from time to time. This is written in the Articles and the Company is bound by this. Naturally, changes can be made by the amendment of the

Articles which will require the approval of the shareholders. A company must give serious consideration to the Board size and composition including diversity as a well-structured Board to assist in ensuring the success of a company. Too small a Board generally does not allow directors to carry out their mandate well as it tends to hamper governance and Boards that are too large tend to be unwieldy, bureaucratic, and slow to make decisions.

Directors should be guided by terms of reference as well as all Committees and Guiding Principles of Governance, including a Directors' Charter are tools to guide the Board in matters such as Board and Committee Term of Office, Rotation, Resignation, Code of Conduct, Disclosures, Indemnifications, Attendance and Remuneration. A Board Charter sets out the Directors' Powers and is a good guide to proper governance, and established its role beyond those that are in the Companies Act or the Articles of Incorporation.

4. Conflict Of Interest

The contract by Directors is a matter that is given serious scrutiny to ensure there is no conflict of interest. A Director, therefore, who is in some way interested in a contract that the

Company has out for tender, should declare his/her interest, and good governance goes further to say he/she should recuse himself/herself from participating in the discussion or voting. In that way, the Director would not have been able to use his/her influence on others to make the final decision.

5. Minutes Of The Meeting

For posterity, proper recording of decisions taken and assistance with the actions arising from meetings whether annual, special or Board meetings, is standard. These Minutes should be circulated on a timely basis, and prior to the next meeting, so that they can be reviewed and where necessary, actions can be effected. All Minutes should be approved by Directors. Specifically, the Minutes should contain the following:

- Appointment of Officers made by Directors.
- The names of the Directors present at each meeting of the Board of Directors and Committees.
- All resolutions taken by the members.
- Only a Director present at that meeting can confirm the Minutes, but it can be seconded by

any Director present at the meeting at which the Minutes are being confirmed.

6. The Role Of The Managing Director

The Managing Director is the highest-ranked Officer of the Company and is an Executive Director. This means that this individual is the head of the management team and is a director on the Board and is allowed to vote on the decisions of the Board. Good corporate governance, as a result, dictates the committees which would conflict with the Managing Director heading or having the power to vote on. The Audit Committee reviews the work of Management and therefore, this would prove a matter of conflict for the Managing Director's presence on the same.

Directors of the Board, based on the Constitutive documents, may have the power from time to time to appoint one of its Directors to be the Managing Director. Where that person ceases to be a Director, his/her power as Managing Director is revoked.

7. Accounting

The litmus test of any organization is usually in the way it keeps its books and records. Many companies see this as a second order of priority until they are ready to access a loan or offer their shares to the public. However, within the Articles of Incorporation, are distinct provisions that Accounts must be kept. The Articles in a section referring to Accounts sets out in simple terms that the Directors shall ensure that proper records are kept of the Company's affairs, and this is not only critical, but it is the essential responsibility of the Board, to ensure that proper records are kept, and that sufficient time is taken by the Board to interrogate management on these records. A country's accountancy Board provides the guidance and standards by which records should be kept and presented to give a true and fair view of the state of the Company's affairs at a given point in time.

The Audit of Accounts

The Board should appoint an Audit Committee mainly comprised of independent directors. They shall be responsible for the review of the monthly financial reports, as well as the Audited Financial Reports as prepared by Management and Independently audited by a recognized audit firm. They must have been appointed by shareholders at an annual general meeting to hold office from the conclusion of that meeting until the conclusion of the next annual general meeting.

It is also recommended that companies establish an internal audit framework and function which can be internal or outsourced with the role of ongoing audit of the organization. This role reports directly to the Board, usually through the Audit Committee.

Measurement Of Directors' Performance – Governance Indicators

Other key considerations to good governance which, if not easily recognizable in the Articles of Incorporation, should consume the attention of the Board of Directors are as follows:

- The rights of shareholders to access information and participate in shareholders' meetings, the ability to approve Board members' compensation, and to review the minutes of Annual General Meetings.

- Whether the company offers ownership rights beyond voting. This typically concerns minority shareholders who believe they are not able to benefit from the company as much as majority shareholders.

- The quality of the Annual Report beyond the basic that is required in the Documents of Incorporation to include well-laid out Management Discussions and Analysis, and information on the performance of each

Board Committee including attendance and frequency of meetings.

- Mechanisms that will allow minority shareholders to influence Board composition.

- The role of the Owner/Influencer, a term that we have used in this book to denote the quiet, hidden power and/or the open power and influence of owners.

- Concentrating on Conflicts of Interest so that the Annual Report provides rationale/explanation for related party transactions affecting the entity.

- Established Communication Portal as an ongoing avenue for updates on the company's performance. These could include websites and other social media avenues.

- Mechanisms for feedback to the Board including whistleblowing policies that should be readily accessible.

- Relationship and communication with stakeholders on matters relating to the environment and social issues.

- Training programmes for Directors on changes to laws and Acts that affect the company in an ever-changing time; matters relating to Cyber Security, Enterprise

Risk Management, Data Privacy, and which impacts the governance of the ownership.

- The disclosure of the company's policies on its website lends itself to transparency of operation.
- Assessment of the Company's performance vis-a-vis its strategic plans.
- The matter of risks represents another level of care that has become even more necessary. As the level of risks, whether internal, external, environmental, or social that face organizations rapidly multiply, good governance becomes more relevant to an entity's growth and sustainability. The emphasis, therefore, that is placed on the creation of policy maintenance and adherence to constitutive documents must be, therefore, ramped up for business survival and transformation. I recommend a Risk Management assurance and insurance program policy that determines and lays out just how the Board will handle risk and liability, both that of the institution and/or organization and its own. Are there policies that indemnify the Directors setting them apart personally from the business operation of the organization that

can protect them from lawsuits while operating in their private capacities?

The Chief Executive Officer (CEO)

The relationship between the Board of Directors, especially the Chairman, and the CEO and the Owner/Influencer (where there is such an identifiable entity) sets the tone for the accomplishment of the mission of the organization and the manifestation of the company's vision. The CEO is the linchpin between the Board, the strategic plan and the organization's operation. Therefore, he or she plays a critical role in the management of the process which includes ensuring that the company adheres to rules, laws, and Articles where applicable, and holds Management accountable for achieving the objectives of the organization.

This is a dynamic role which is called on to understand the role as strategic thinker, conceptualizer, knowledge builder, and performance assessor. These can only be possible if he/she upholds critical governance principles and standards and has systems in place to evaluate the effectiveness of these standards. While the CEO represents the operational arm of the Board and guide its Chair to set the navigation sights in order, attention must be given to the political realities of the Owner/Influencer in the hold of the ship.

We speak to standards, but they change daily and sometimes minutely depending on external conditions, government policies, or even strategic shifts in the organization or an industry. Therefore, the CEO must be flexible and adaptable with ears to the ground, nose to the grind, heart attuned, and head programmed to be receptive and willing to distill information and distinguish between those actions which would be classified as not within the scope of good governance and those that will elevate the company.

There should be full transparency between the Chief Executive Officer and the Board. Consequently, there should be an agreed mode of communication between the Board and the CEO, which will include a dashboard of strategies and initiatives, and a measurement of progress. In many organizations, this is effected through the Balanced Score Card Method, which reports using four perspectives, namely: learning and growth, business processes, customer perspectives, and financial data. Recently, software has been developed to enhance Board communication, and many Boards now possess the same. These legs, as they are called, are what make up the visions and strategies we previously discussed. It is through these limbs, legs, hands, feet, eyes, and ears, that the CEO reports to the Board, which shares the same expectations and priorities, thereby allowing for successful evaluation of programmes and outcomes based on predetermined metrics.

Globally, risks have become more pervasive as the world becomes more digital. The steps into the organization and key responsibilities of the CEO are to manage several types of risks such as Business Risks, Strategic Risks and Hazard Risks. Arising out of those, certain more defined risk types are Cyber Security, Enterprise Risk, and Data Privacy Risk. This is a mammoth task, but the CEO's responsibility is to ensure that the organization is well resourced, whether through outsourcing or having the necessary cadre of staff and technology to appropriately measure and manage these risks.

The reputation of the organization is extrinsically and intrinsically tied to the reputation of the CEO which makes him or her one of the major risk factors of the organization. It is, therefore, necessary to foster full transparency between the Board and the CEO in matters relating to external business affairs that could impact the company and internal business affairs that could impact the CEO in his normal life.

Therefore, an agreed Code of Ethics for the Board, CEO, and employees, is an excellent platform on which to build trust, understanding and transparency. The CEO must help in crafting and communicating the organization's values up and down the ladder and to third parties.

Leadership exists at all levels of the organization. The CEO is, however, the leader-in-chief who must lead from the front, test the waters, uphold the highest standards of good governance, and establish his/ her credibility to both managers, employees, and the Board. This must be done by demonstrating his/her understanding of corporate policies and procedures and displaying a commitment not to sidestep these whether through expediency or for personal interest. It is through the leadership of the CEO that Boards are deemed to be successful, and it is with the open relationship and dialogue with the Board that the CEO is primarily viewed as being a success. Let us not forget about the informal influencer/power structure that is a characteristic of many situations. Critical, therefore, to the success of the organization, is the proper synergy between the CEO and the Board, the understanding of each person's role and responsibility, the agreement that good governance exists where there are demarcations of these roles and a healthy and agreed means of measurement and accountability.

Chapter 4

Towards Synergetic Alignment— Board, CEO, And Influencer

Towards Synergetic Alignment—Board, CEO, And Influencer

"Can Three Walk Together, Except They Be Agreed?"

"*Houston, we have a problem.*" The Chairman of the Spacecraft Board of Governors, the CEO and Owner, Mellone Luske, are all wondering how to redirect the path of the outgoing spacecraft that is headed to Jupiter instead of Mars, as we earlier decided." The two men and one woman, respectively, Board Chair, CEO and "Owner/Influencer", hail from different countries and cultures and have diverse perspectives on governance and have much at stake. "The Owner/Influencer has put trillions into Houston Central, while the Board Chair is beholden to several other investors, and the CEO to all the ground crew, performing the actual operations. How can we identify the present dilemma, and create aligned synergy to determine the best structure, strategy, and program to direct this spacecraft to Mars with our diversity, equity, and inclusion?"

I am persuaded that it is of paramount importance to gain congruence, a purposeful direction, a meaningful strategy, and a structural mechanism, that is sensitive to culture and context. In this chapter, therefore, we introduce the concept of the triad/trio, rather than the dyad/duo (the traditional Board Chair and CEO-Espoused Theory). The governance triad portrays the flow of communication between three entities—the CEO, the Board Chair, and the "Owner", hereinafter understood as the "Owner/Influencer". The assumption is that, in a governance model, while we portray a Board Chair-CEO dynamic in corporate circles, there is always a powerful third party, a "silent" owner-type, that influences both Board Chair and CEO.

We use "owner/influencer" to denote an individual of authority and influence either through resources, or political authority and power, who may or may not be on the Board, but who exerts considerable persuasive influence. We have labelled this structure, as an integrated democratic-political model in which there are three personalities operative, rather than two, thus, our geometrical shape. This is the hidden force in corporatocracy where we define owner (silent force and/or leader), the one Board member with the finance or any informal individual outside of the CEO and Board Chair, and that hidden force which I call "Owner/Influencer". The question now becomes, "Can three walk together except they be agreed, and aligned?" The Board_Chair represents the interests of the Board, and its stakeholders; the CEO represents the operating interests and functions of the company in its daily operations; and the financial owner/influencer of the Company, who may or may not appear as part of the formal structure but can exert quiet and hidden influence and interests through de facto or de jure ownership. Is your situation geometrical, a two-sided dyad, or a three-sided triad?

● ● ●

History, Context & Culture

We face a challenge in corporate governance systems, as we struggle with the present, inherited historical structure, to create a synergy between Board chairs and executive teams. How do we create eloquent, effective, and efficient synergies that will materialize into productivity in an age of uncertainty, technological creativity, and a society that encourages diverse opinions and disruptive thought? What we inherit often determines our philosophy and how we govern, thus, our destiny. At best, governance in the Americas and the developing Western world represents a compromised balancing act between the governed and those governing, stemming from the early national constitutional enablement of freedom and balance between the stakeholders holding ultimate sway through a representative democracy of voice and vote. It is the ongoing clash of the center versus the periphery, of rulers versus peasants, and plantation owners versus field workers. Present governance systems arise out of our practice of a democracy where all classes are represented in a trend away from aristocracy and dictatorship toward a position of shared and representative governance, that invites diverse opinions and ideas so that all voices are heard.

This chapter quotes the oft-used phrase, "Can two walk together except they be agreed," into the new phrase, "Can three walk together," for three pairs of hands, devolving into six hands might be the new pictorial and structural order of the day. That is, can the Board, the CEO Executive team, and the "Owner/Influencer", make joint progress, except they are agreed on the directional destination, and the strategy for getting there and the resources, whether personnel or financial, to enable the completed journey? This is the question that paves the way for synergistic goal alignment between the CEO and the Board chair, into a triune being. "Can Three Walk Together Except they be Agreed?" The organization becomes philosophically driven through a compromise of shared governance mix representing a mix of autocracy, and bureaucracy, democracy, and socialism, with active movement from right to center to left, and vice versa.

We gather this concept from that historical treatise called, "The Separation of Powers", the realization that there is power and that the King should never hold full sway — the King reigns in his palace; the Judges reign in their judiciary and the people elect them occasionally and leave everyday operations to be monitored by their representatives. Rather than "separate the powers", shall we not now, "balance the powers", for integration, collaboration, and cooperation?

Success Requirement — An Alignment

Success is based on the alignment of intangibles, tangibles, and a power grid as critical ingredients, as we lay out these variables beside each other in welcome alignment. The intangibles of trust, respect, confidence, and relationships are important elements to Board-CEO synergies that lead to clearer vision and strategy. The tangibles of measurable results, periodic bottom-line information and accountability to shareholders, investors, and constituents, are part of the clear expectations that the stakeholder leaders must incorporate. Shared power and influence are other aspects of the equation. Expert power is born from knowledge and experience; referent power speaks to the support the triad has from stakeholders and legal power flows from the Constitution and the Bylaws. The combination of these power sources gives rise to status or positional power. The power grid must then be aligned within the triad of Board Chair, CEO, and "Owner-Influencer" with a clear determination of boundaries, responsibilities, and accountability.

This alignment of power, intangibles and tangibles now prepares the organization for the determination, definition and clarification of roles and expectations.

The Behavioral Expectations of the Parties
Role of the Board & Chair

The role of the Board and its Chair lies in strategic visioning, hiring, and evaluation of the CEO, oversight, and stakeholder representation, to keep the organization on track toward its destination in a fiduciary and confident manner. The Board is also legally responsible for the decisions made, and in the new AI world, the matter of Board technological software serves to protect critical Board information.

Again, the question arises, "Can three walk together", except there is a common agreement about philosophy, direction, and strategy? Who does and is responsible for what becomes critically important so no one area overrides the other? When the CEO gets a 'directive' from the Owner/Influencer, yet another from the Board Chair, and yet another trending from senior fellow administrators, it demonstrates that it is time for the alignment of the vehicle tires and if you would like, tiers. Again, our thesis in this chapter is that there is a triad, not a dyad. A number of complementary roles emerge. Here is a dyadic representation which can be extrapolated to include a third dimension.

Table 1 – Board Chair/CEO Role Clarifications

Our theme here is that there must be an alignment where each group understands the clear roles and expectations of the other.

Board Chair	CEO
Chairs the Board	Leads the Company
Broad Picture — Long term	Operations Management
Stakeholders	Strategy Implementer
Collective Power	Executive Power
Seeks Information	Keeps the Board informed
Strategy & Oversight, Insight, Hindsight, Foresight	Combining these sights into creative action around a working team
Sounding Board	Sounding Board
Evaluates the Executive Team	Evaluates employees
Passionate	Passionate
Resource gathering	Resource gathering
Joint Consultation	Joint Consultation
Decides legal directions	Makes recommendations — does the homework
Accountable to the shareholders	Accountable to the Board and provides regular reports

Financial oversight, Asset protection, Fiduciary, Audit Committee Sub-committees: Select, support, and review the performance, Recruiting new boards members Care, loyalty, confidentiality No conflict of interests Commitment of time, integrity, welcoming to diverse views.	Financial reporting, places relevant administrator or individual on sub-committees in advisory capacity. Reviews internal performance, Speaks on behalf of the institution, No conflict of interests, commitment of time; integrity; welcomes diverse views.

Table 2 – The Ten Cs of Boards and Organizations

These prescriptions enable all parties to be responsible.
The aim here is to gain congruence to attain positive
alignment between the parties.

Category	Description
Conduct	Ethical behaviors
Communication	Talk in terms understood
Collaboration	Work with groups
Consultation	Seek opinions and advice
Clarification	Clear up dark spots
Creation	Birth new ideas
Confidentiality	Ability to repose in each other
Codification	Constitution & Bylaws
Consecration	Dedication to the task
Calibration	Adaptability and resilience

Table 3 –The Four Board and CEO Sights

Board Chair, CEO and Owner (where applicable) must understand and align on the following sights.

Hindsight	Review of history that can impact the present experience
Oversight	Reviewing targets and performance
Insight	Opportunity exploration in the present
Foresight	Scenario creation and visioning to prepare for the future

Board-CEO-Owner Dilemmas

The three-some will face some dilemmas and wisdom calls to track and identify these dilemmas in the early continuing constants for resolution. Once there is uncertainty and rapid change in the environment, dilemmas will be present. Dilemmas are opportunities for growth and success:

1. Distraction vs Attention – the urgent versus the important.

2. Diversity vs Inclusion – gender, ethnicity, ideas.

3. Power-sharing – who has the power.

4. The Pilate Syndrome – the matter of who is accountable.

5. The Short vs the Long Term – the daily versus the annual.

6. Tenure – when to step away - shelf-life determinations.

Again, the issue of alignment arises. How do we include the dilemmas in the equation of intangibles, tangibles, success requirements, power, and roles? What we have developing is a series of independent variables related to the success (the dependent variable) of the enterprise. In statistical research terms, the following diagram is used as a predictable equation where the interaction of the independent Y variables impacts the outcome of the X variable.

● ● ●

Toward Alignment — An Illustration

Independent and dependent variables are integral to Board/CEO success. An independent variable is a factor or matter that impacts a desired result, and a dependent variable is the desired result to be predicted. Each independent variable (Y1, Y2, Y3, Y4, Y5) impacts and influences the dependent variable (X (Board and organizational success)). What is desired is the alignment of the Y variables in such a manner that success is assured on the X variable. It is the strength of the alignment that will determine the rate of success. This model must be carefully understood by the principal parties.

Table 4 – Representation of Independent and Dependent Variables.

This figure portrays the schematic operation of the Y and X variables. The Y factors can impact the X factor and demonstrate which of the Y variables causes the greatest variance with X.

X – Success	Y1- Intangibles	Y2 Tangibles	Y3 Power	Y4 Structure	Y5 Roles
Matter 1	I1	T1	P1	S1	R1
Matter 2	I2	T2	P2	S2	R2
Matter 3	I3	T3	P3	S3	R3
Matter 4	I4	T4	P4	S4	R4

Initial Environmental Scan

Again, the following steps call for alignment and understanding at all levels as to what the Board is expected to approve, and the CEO expected to recommend. It is the job of the CEO to recommend, and the duty of the Board to approve and/or disapprove recommendations. A recommendation that comes to the Board from the CEO does not arrive naked and unclothed. It has arrived through consultation, conversation, and prior collaboration. The Board may also make recommendations in consultation and alignment. Too often, CEOs take problems to Boards without any clear recommended course of action. Here are some useful steps:

1. Assessment:
    a. Assess the environment and the industry to determine the competitive framework in which the company or organization must exist. What type of company are you — a fringe upstart firm, a company that has had a monopoly on a service or product, or an oligopolistic company where you are one of the powerhouses? Is your environment harsh, uncertain, or predictable?

    b. Determine a vision — what is the destination?

    c. Identify the stakeholders — who are the customers?

    d. Understand the history of governance — what have been the traditions?

2. Determine Board structure and role:

    a. Clarify the roles of Board.

    b. Establish a Constitution and By-laws and a method of governance.

    c. Determine the relevant Legal and Financial Requirements.

    d. Initiate and implement.

3. Measure and Evaluate for Quality and Goal Achievement

Takeaways

Here are some helpful takeaways to ponder:

1. Context and History: We derive our present governance structure from history, context, and culture. In any instance, a Board and CEO are wise to study this variable as it embarks on its mission.

2. Board Power Structure: Contrary to popular belief and practice in some areas, the Board power structure is not

a duo, but a trio (dyad versus triad) consisting of the Board Chair, the CEO, and the Chief "Owner/ Influencer".

3. Impacting Factors: There is an independent/ dependent variable framework that can impact the success of organizations—many factors interact to determine successful outcomes.

4. Mantras and Prescriptions: The Board, CEO and "Owner/Influencer" should identify, describe, and then align a number of mantras and prescriptions.

5. The Horns of a Dilemma: Dilemmas welcome opportunities for creative solutions; identify them and then prepare.

6. Alignment: The parties in power must have alignment in role and function, the sharing of power, the positioning of tangibles and intangibles. I am persuaded to advocate for an "Alignment Manual".

Can, *"Three walk together except they be agreed?"* The real true work of a Board and organization is to look at and plan for the future with an eye on the present, for it is the future very often that determines the present. The future represents that great unknown. Instead of waiting for the future, the Board,

CEO and "Owner/Influencer" must create and dream that future through the discussion and tabling of various "if—then" scenarios with a plan for each. While this is happening, we can watch the store. Do not try to be like everyone else- be yourself and distinguish your organization from every other.

Issue at Stake—Departure and Transitioning

Leadership, at Best, is a Relay Race of Passing the Baton Board members, Chairs, Chief Executive Officers, and owners may need to step aside, step down, retire, and depart for a multitude of reasons. The manner of execution can significantly impact reputation, brand, and ongoing operations. _To not know, that you do not know, spells disaster!_

1. How should Board members, owners, and CEOs prepare to leave office? — A departure should not place the Board or organization in jeopardy

   - In a professional manner with a written letter or public announcement, earlier communicated to the Board, that satisfies all legal requirements and fiduciary responsibilities.
   - In the case of owners, provide for the appropriate transfers, as required.

- Set up an internal continuation mechanism.
- Sign no legal documents in the last 60 days that could bind the Board without a second signature.
- Ensure that there are onboarding procedures for incoming members.
- Arrange a formal exit report and meeting with the Board.
- Leave quietly and without fanfare.

2. What can the president do to transfer leadership to the next generation? Do not stop planning!
   - Select a broad range of strategies for positivity.
   - Arrange leadership succession planning guidelines.
   - Transfer leadership begins on the president's 1st day through wise delegating and skill-building among associates.
   - Ensure that all systems are well-tuned and working.
   - Develop a transition onboarding manual.

3. Beyond term limits, why is it important to know the right time to say goodbye?

- Match capability with environment and strength.

- The environment is one of constant change which may require different strategies that play to the strengths of leaders.

- Leaders should be aware of the match between their strengths and organizational needs — some leaders are visionary and others, implementers. The relay race, baton-passing strategy, is the goal toward completion of the institutional vision. Get on board.

Chapter 5

A Handy Directors' Companion

A Handy Directors' Companion A-Z

Since Good Governance is an absolute necessity for growth, this chapter provides a compendium of common terms and actions or feelings that are associated with governance from A-Z.

> *"Think, grow, act with values, and deliver worth."* (Dr. Isaac Newton, 2023).
>
> *"Vision is where you are going, and mission is what you are doing. What you are doing is where you are going, and where you are going is what you are doing. If you don't determine where you are going, what you are doing becomes meaningless."* (Dr. Sylvan Lashley, 2023).
>
> *"Concepts and definitions are powerful tools for those who are embracing good governance thinking and practices. By recognizing the scarce commodity of 'time', this ready reckoner provides a quick point of reference for a better understanding of every situation."* (Dr. Marlene Street Forest, 2023).

A

Alignment	The blending of purpose of the organization with its mission and vision.
Acceptance	Agreement with the unanimous or majority decision of the Board.
Accountability	Accepting responsibility for your action and the collective action of the Board.
Audit	A check to determine that the company adheres to established standards and procedure. An Audit Committee of the Board is essential to good governance.

B

Board	The composition of directors that fit the purpose of the organization. It is best when there is a combination of non-independent and independent directors considering diversity in age, gender, and race.
Benefits of Board	Sets strategic direction and focuses on strategic outcome; holds Management accountable; and network for the benefit of the organization.

Board Management Software	Software that enables Boards to conduct business in privacy, aided by technology.

C

Company Secretary	The individual at the Board with many responsibilities such as sending out the Notice for AGM, organizing company meetings, ensuring the company complies with regulations, etc.
Culture	The tone at the top which is set by the Board, driven by management and filters through the organization.
Chairperson	Responsible for smoothly guiding the Board's discussions and decisions in keeping with its mission and vision and strategic direction.
Conflict of Interest	Official document which Board members sign to declare that they have no competing and/or conflicting personal or business interests that could affect the manner in which to vote and behave in a

	negative manner toward the Board and the organization.
CEO	Chief Executive Officer—individual who presides over the organization and represents the Board to the organization.
Confidentiality NDA—Non-Disclosure Agreement	Signed statement by Board members declaring the limits of disclosure on which they all agree, so that private matters of the Board are held inviolate and non-disclosed to third parties.
Creating Shared Value	Engaging in initiatives that permit organizations to make a profit in ways that are socially beneficial and acceptable by recipients.
Corporate Social Responsibility	Participating in programs with the aim of producing social good that aligns with an organization's mission, and which can yield positive relations.

D

Discretion	The use of knowledge, experience and wisdom when addressing critical issues of the Board. An appreciation that

	independence of thought is essential to arriving at the best decision.
Details	While Boards must not delve into minutia, some detailed information critical to the company's profitability such as financial reports are necessary for Board scrutiny and discussion.
Delegation	Boards function optimally where there are sub-committees which the Board empowers to fulfill certain responsibilities and provide oversight and feedback. Examples of these are the Risk Committee, the Audit Committee., Remuneration Committee and Corporate Governance Committee.
Duties	The directors of the Board are bound by the Articles of Incorporation and/or other constitutive documents of the company. The main duties of directors include setting strategies, holding management accountable, ensuring that the policies are maintained, and that there is due diligence in operation. The Board is NOT

	management and must not assume the role of management, which is to deliver operationally.
Duty of Care	Board members are required to adhere to a specific standard of what a reasonable person would do to avoid careless acts that could foreseeably harm the company.
Duty of Loyalty	A requirement that each Board member puts the interests of the Board and organization before his/her own personal interests.
Duty of Obedience	The Board member must comply with and adhere to all legal provisions as per applicable laws and regulations that accord with its own policies.
De Jure	Legal and Board authorization to perform certain functions as a right.
De Facto	A Board member acting in a certain capacity, but not officially appointed for the same.

E

Empathy	A Board needs a soul. Members should, within the construct of good governance, be able to empathize with management on issues such as unexpected occurrence in operations and environmental matters affecting the organization.
Evaluation of Organization	Board documents must be received in a manner that allows for the evaluation of business against key performance matrix, budget versus actual performance, environmental mapping and analysis, and visual representation including charts and graphs.
Evaluation of Board and CEO	Evaluation of directors should be conducted at least annually with the overall Board, including peer and self-evaluation. The Chair has the responsibility to ensure that each director is held for his performance on the Board.
Excuse, Absence & Apology	At times, directors will find it necessary to be absent from meetings. Directors are required to send an apology to the

	Company Secretary. Although most constitutive documents will not prescribe the number of meetings at which a director should be present annually, directors should try to be present at least 70% of the time.
Ethics	A system of values leading to conduct as adopted by the Board.

F

Financial Reports	Financial Probity is extremely important. Directors should pay keen attention to these reports and ensure that at least one board member has the necessary audit and financial experience to analyze the financial report as tabled by management. The Audit Committee must be tasked to examine the financial statements of the Board on a monthly or bi-monthly basis and provide a report and recommendation to the Board.
Fixed Date	The Company Secretary should fix the dates of Board meetings for a calendar year to

	ensure that directors can plan meetings, and management can prepare documents to reach the Board at a predetermined time to allow directors to prepare.
Frequency of Meetings	To ensure relevance and time to deal with matters affecting the company, including corrective measures, Board meetings should be held at least six (6) times annually.
Filings	Annual Returns and Financials must be filed with the relevant government authority.
Fiduciary	A Board member who is required and expected to act in the best interests of the Board and/or the beneficiary and not their own interests and is ethically and legally liable for the same.

G

Governance	This is the responsibility of the Board- to provide the framework which will allow directors and management to operate in a fair, ethical, and accountable environment.

Gender	A fair gender mix is important to allow for differing views and perspectives.

H

High Impact Behaviour	This involves the following factors: (a) Be prepared and engaged. (b) Be fully present at meetings avoiding multi-tasking. (c) Add value to the discussion. (d) Be the subject matter expert.
Habit	Make a habit of reading Board reports and asking pertinent questions. Do not excessively dominate meetings.
History	Especially for new directors, have a proper orientation programme. The history of the organization matters. Know the business, its foundation and growth including past successes and failures. Participate and contribute to the annual report which is usually a compendium of the company's operation in any given year.

I

Intellectual Property	Ensure that the company's intellectual property, trademarks and trade names are protected through copyright.
Integrity	Directors must ensure that they are honest with the dealings of their own personal affairs as well as the company's, as either can affect the reputation of the other. Declare matters that can be considered conflict of interest.
Institutional Framework	The Board must ensure that the institutional framework of the company is developed. These include Board charter and policies that govern the company's operations. These documents must always be approved, signed, and dated by the Board and reviewed periodically in keeping with the policy for review.

J

Justice	Justice requires general concern and respect for people. A Board is elevated when members show respect for each other in

	language, space to comment and to share perspective.

K

Knowledge	Directors must keep current on issues that may affect them as a director and the company, for example, issues regarding legislative changes, or regulatory requirements. Knowledge of these is critical to governance and annual training should be conducted to ensure directors are current.

L

Length of tenure	Directors' length of tenure is important to Boards. While all Boards do well because of stability, refreshing the Board is an important part of governance.
Loneliness	A director must be prepared at some time to be lonely if he/she has a dissenting view. These are sometimes constructive avenues for Board growth or organization pivoting which needs to be voiced and discussed.

Legal Documents	The Articles of Incorporation is the principal legal document for the company and the duties of directors are contained therein.
Legal Obligations	Certain legal obligations that directors must fulfil include the filing of audited financial statements and the payment of statutory deductions and corporation taxes. These should be reported on by management along with the financial reports.

M

Mission Statement	The company's mission statement should be like the National Anthem to directors. It should be studied, known, and understood. The statement is action based and establishes the agreed purpose of the organization and its objectives in service to its customers. It declares the company's raison d'etre.
Management	The Managing Director is a director of the Board and holds the most senior executive position of the Company. Non-executive

	directors are not managers and should not assume the role of management.
Meetings - General	The Company Secretary is required to arrange meetings of the Board. Meetings must be quorate for them to be legitimately recorded as meetings of the Board. Meetings must have the following character: • An agenda • Place, Date and Time • Quorate – meaning that a minimum number of members required for meetings are there to begin and continue the meeting through to its termination. • Directors must approve minutes. • The Directors should approve Variation of Agenda. • An individual who was not at the minutes of the meeting at which he/she was not present. Director can however second those minutes.

Meetings – Annual	Under the provisions of most constitutive documents this must be held annually, giving shareholders the opportunity to receive the audited financial statements of the company, hear the auditors' opinions of the company, ask questions of the Board of Directors and Management on the discharge of their functions, and to receive Management's Discussion and Analysis. Shareholders vote on the Financial Statements, the directorship, and their remuneration, matters of capitalization, and the audit firm.
Mentorship	Critical process in director's orientation where a director is introduced and 'shadow' a more seasoned director.

N

News	Discussions at the Board are not company news which fits the normal approved process for Communication to shareholders and stakeholders.

	Discussions at the Board should be kept confidential by all directors unless it is agreed that this should be disseminated. A communication policy is critical to good governance.
Networking	Networking is a primary responsibility of the directors. They should hone these skills as it increases knowledge of the industry and helps to address problems and opportunities which can and will present themselves.
Non-Executive Director	A non-executive director is a member of the Board but does not form part of the executive or management team.

O

Organize	Directors need to organize themselves and their time so that they understand what is driving the business, deal with mission critical issues, read and understand the minutes, and act where necessary to improve the net worth of the company.

Orientation	Good governance dictates that all directors must undergo a period of orientation to allow for knowledge of the business, people, and mission.
Oversight	The continuous accountability system whereby the Board sets up a system to receive periodic reports from the CEO on progress toward strategic goals and the state of operations.

P

Policies	Organizations benefit from clear policies which are driven by the mission of the company and other legal and legislatives requirements. Policies build the framework of an organization and protect the rights of all stakeholders. Policies may include governance, sexual harassment, Code of Ethics, and Workplace Safety and Health. The Board must approve all policies.

Protection	Regarding the level of responsibilities of Directors, the Board should consider Directors & Officers Liability Insurance policy. This protects the personal assets of corporate Directors and Officers in the event a Director is sued for actual or alleged or wrongful act in managing a company.

Q

Quality Assurance	A Director should inspect what to expect. The Audit Committee should ensure that matters of quality control and assurance are met throughout the organization, typically by the direct report of the internal auditors.
Quantifiable Action	Where tasks or operations are quantifiable these reports should be provided to the Board and include budget, profit, return on investment, and other ratios.

R

Results	Directors should require of management positive results, not only measured by profitability but should also include information such as: • Staff turnover ratio • Management letters from Auditors • Staff Training and • Customer Surveys
Retreat	The Board of Directors must retreat. It is preferable that this is done annually. Retreats are meant to provide a means where the board can assess, discuss, and align the future strategies for growth and recommit to the vision of the organization.
Risk Management	Critical to the sustainability of the company, directors must interrogate senior management about risks affecting the directors including enterprise risks, environmental risks, and cybersecurity risk. A Board must decide the company's

	risk tolerance, strategies, and business models.
Relationship	Building good relationships with fellow Board members and management is critical to Board cohesion and results.

S

Success	Directors succeed when each is invested in the company, understands the vision, is inspired to inspire others, vests operations to management and holds them responsible, is prepared to listen, is open to other's ideas, measures performance and assesses risks.
Strategies	'Culture eats strategy for breakfast.' Directors must ensure that the strategies contemplated to meet the goals and objectives are in tune with the mission and vision of the company and that these strategies are organizational culture appropriate. Managing time, resources, and conflicts are important considerations in strategic planning and management.

T

Training	Directors should invest in self-training even though the company invests in ensuring directors are kept abreast with appropriate training.
Trust	The element of trust is critical to Board cohesion and management effectiveness. Trust improves quality of discussion, reduces time for decision making, and improve board/management relationship.
Transparency	This is defined as a state where there are no secrets which will deleteriously affect the organization and could lead to internal or public mistrust. The directors should ensure that the organization's structure is not opaque or lends itself to silos.

U

Unbridled Power	A heavy balance is the composition of the Board which can lead to unbridled power where majority decisions are taken drowning out the views and objection of

	other directors. Independent vs. non-independent directors.

V

Values & Attitude	A system of individual beliefs and philosophies adopted by a Board to guide action and behavior.
Vision	A statement that clearly states what the organization is becoming and hopes to become—its destination point.

W

Whistleblowing	Mechanism and policy should be effected to allow directors to get information that could help in determining the organization's management or operation in a structured and independent way.
Window Dressing	Any action that tends to alter an object or item to have it appear in a much more superfluous light than ordinary.

X

Extra Special Perception	Directors must develop a sixth (6th) sense which allows for additional probity or scrutiny of matters that could impact the Board. These may be internal or external to the company.

Y

Youthful Board	A youthful Board does not necessarily have anything to do with age but rather with mindset. A successful Board is required to have a current mindset which allows decisions to be conceptualized, operationalized, tracked or fast tracked, or delayed, depending on current circumstances in the company or environment.
Ying & Yang	Ying -Directors must ensure that the message or messaging is structured and understood. Yang- Not all things will be black & white so the spiritual and softer skills must be honed for complete assessment and decision making.

Z

Zero Tolerance	There must be zero tolerance for anything that violates established corporate governance, as non-compliance can lead to reputational damage, destruction of public trust, and confidence which is costly to any organization.

About the Authors

Dr. Marlene Street Forrest, CD, JP, is Managing Director of the Jamaica Stock Exchange, and a renowned financial expert, and Author of the book *On Leadership Discipline, Discretion and Daring.* She is the recipient of the prestigious Order of Distinction in the Rank of Commander (CD) and from Canada, the Afro-Global Excellence Award for Global Impact.

Dr. Sylvan Lashley is a strategic leadership specialist, former President of Northern Caribbean University (Jamaica, West Indies), University of Southern Caribbean (Trinidad, West Indies) and the former Atlantic Union College (Massachusetts, USA), as well as a parochial school superintendent in New York. He has served on several boards and is the President of SALCA, Inc.

Dr. Isaac Newton is a versatile expert specializing in change management, crisis intervention, strategic solutions, campaign design, and transformational leadership. He advises high-profile leaders in government, business, academia, and religion on achieving success through utilizing mission-focused approaches, conflict resolution, harnessing uncertainty, navigating boards, and rebranding. As an author of multiple books, Dr. Newton inspires others to leverage wisdom from wounds. He is the president of Paramount Communication & Marketing, LLC.

Made in the USA
Columbia, SC
24 September 2024

42229623R00059